22.05.99.

Dear Charles,

Happy B-day
this book is meant to be an
inspiration!

God Bless
Angela

THE BOOK OF

JONAH

NEWLY REVISED

BY

R. O. BLECHMAN

PART ONE

"Clearly," thought God, disguised as a scotch pine sapling, "these are the wickedest people I have ever seen. The wickedest." He was in the central square of Nineveh, a great city in the land of Babylon.

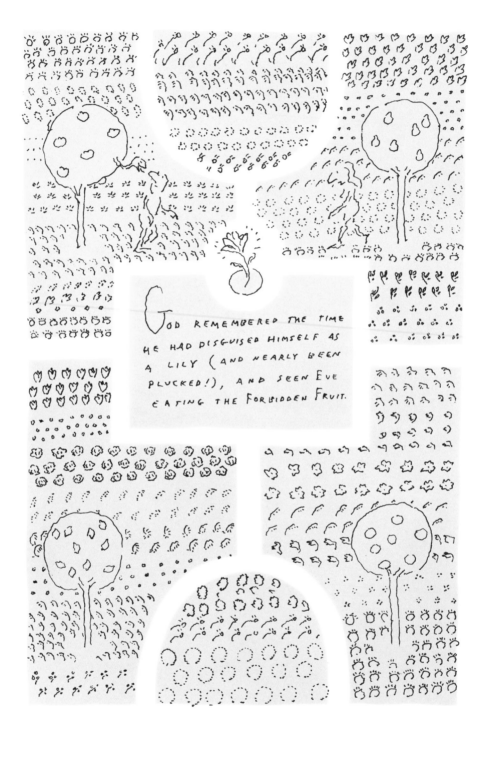

GOD REMEMBERED THE TIME HE HAD DISGUISED HIMSELF AS A LILY (AND NEARLY BEEN PLUCKED!), AND SEEN EVE EATING THE FORBIDDEN FRUIT.

HE REMEMBERED THE FIRST MURDER,
WHEN CAIN KILLED ABEL, ...

GOD AS A WHITE ROSE

HE REMEMBERED THE DAYS
BEFORE THE GREAT FLOOD, ...

GOD AS A STORM CLOUD

HE REMEMBERED THE ENSLAVEMENT
OF THE JEWS BY EGYPT, ...

GOD AS A
BURNING BUSH

HE REMEMBERED
(TO HIS REGRET.
IT WAS A MOMENT
OF WRATH)
WHEN HE DESTROYED
SODOM AND
GOMORROH —

(THE CHILDREN,
HE THOUGHT,
WHO DID NOT KNOW
THEIR LEFT HANDS
FROM THEIR
RIGHT!)

GOD HURLING HIS CAIN-RAISER LIGHTNING BOLT.

He remembered all this,
and far more, ...

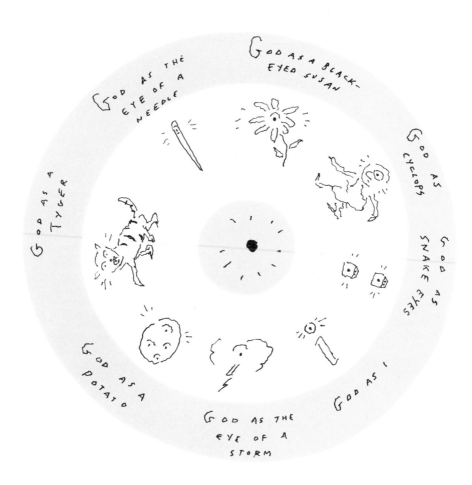

But Never had he seen anything as wicked as the citizens of Nineveh. Never.

"I MUST FIND SOMEBODY TO SPEAK OUT AGAINST THIS WICKEDNESS," HE THOUGHT.

MEANWHILE,
IN NABATEA, ...

"AND IN CONCLUSION, MY FRIENDS,
LET US REMEMBER THAT THIS LAND OF
OURS — THIS BEACON OF COMMERCE
AND CULTURE — THIS LIGHTHOUSE OF
LEARNING IN STORM-TOSSED TIMES
— CAN ONLY STAND AS LONG AS
ITS FOUNDATIONS OF JUSTICE AND
BROTHERHOOD REMAIN STRONG.
GOD BLESS YOU ALL."

What a day! This morning I sold 120 yards of fancy linen, and this evening — a Great speech to the Nabatean Junior Boosters!

Now I'll write up the books!

Here. Some hot soup.

120 yards linen, 14.50. 30 silk shawls, 12.20 And this is the 13th nissan...

It's getting cold...

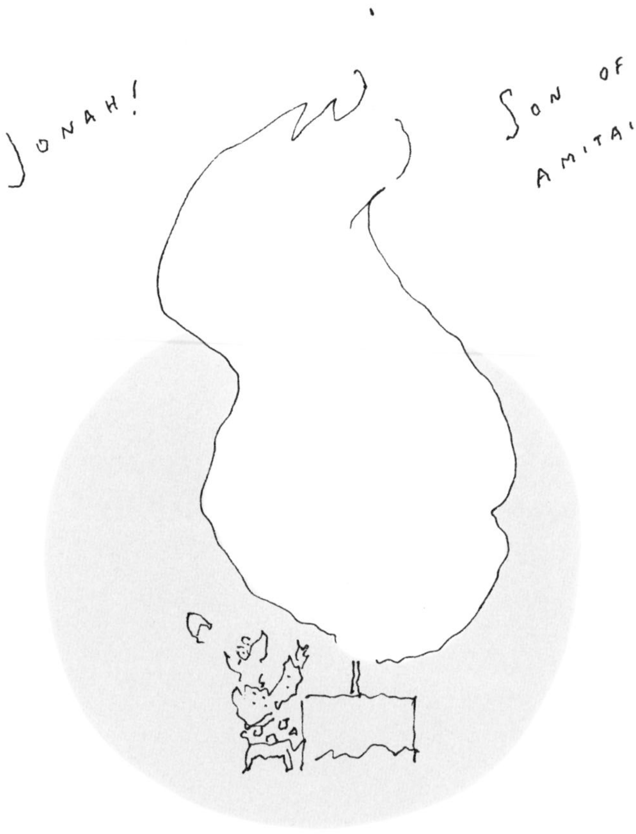
JONAH!
SON OF AMITAI!

who's there?
IT IS I THE LORD THY GOD
GOD OF THY FATHER AND GOD OF THY FATHER'S FARTHEST FATHER.
YES Lord?

I HAVE COME TO COMMAND THEE ARISE, PACK THY BELONGINGS TAKE THEE TO NINEVEH THAT GREAT CITY AND CRY AGAINST IT FOR ITS WICKEDNESS!

NOW ??

Are you sure
you have the
right Jonah, Lord?
There are lots of
Jonahs, you know...

There's Jonah Cohen,
just down the street.
And Jonah... You know,
what's his name again?...

JONAH SON
OF AMITAI

COMMAND
THEE !

Lord?

Hello,
Lord ??

Lord???

PART
TWO

N · A · B · A

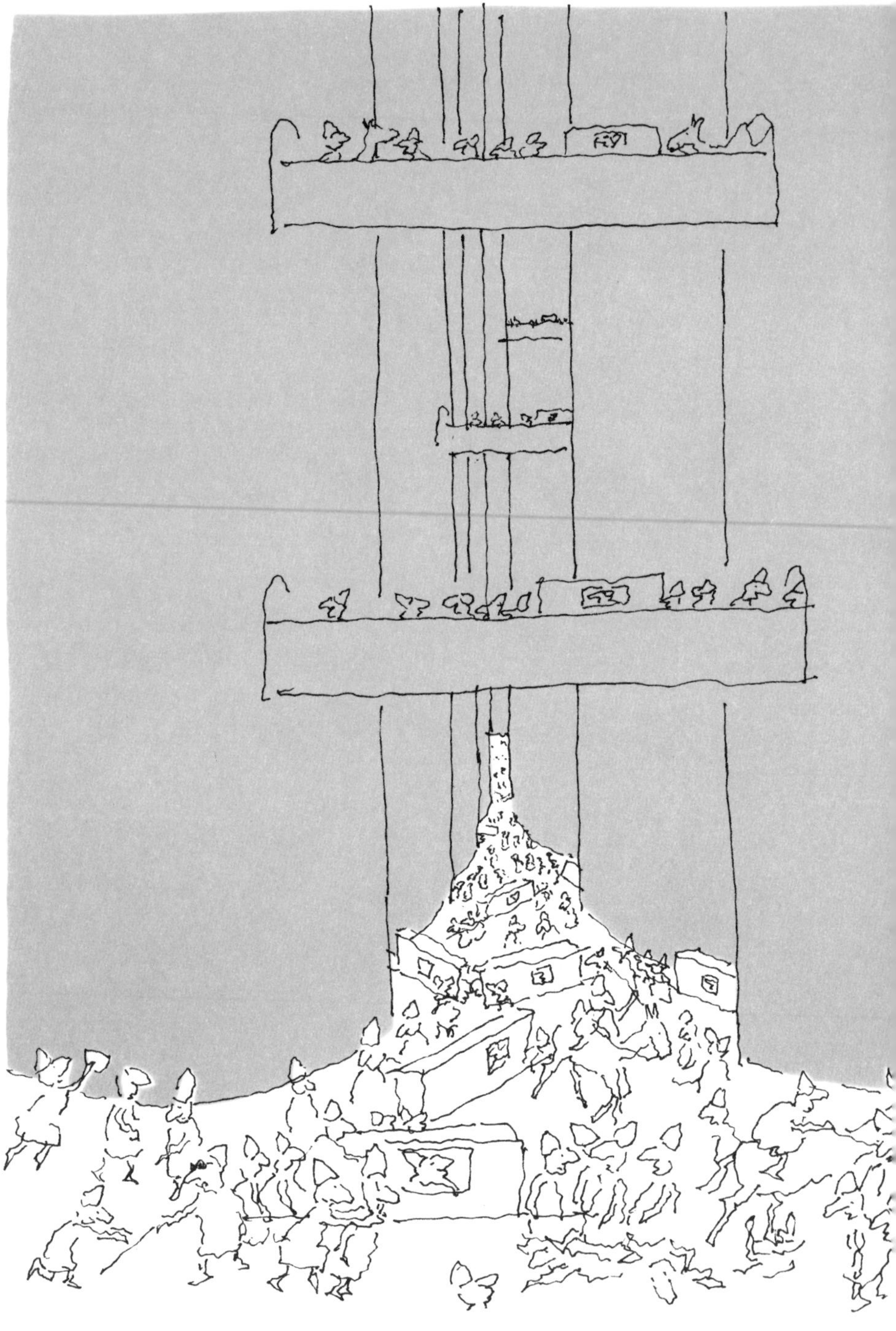

I should have been a vagrant. God would have chosen somebody else!
CAREFUL WITH THAT TREASURE CHEST!!
A tall tree attracts lightning. But a shrub... ...who notices??
SS TARSHISH

It's getting rough, Captain!

Take down the sail, men
AYE, AYE, CAPTAIN!

Batten the hatches!
AYE, AYE, CAPTAIN!
Tighten the winches!
What's a winch?
I think he said wench.
Well, there's that funny lady...

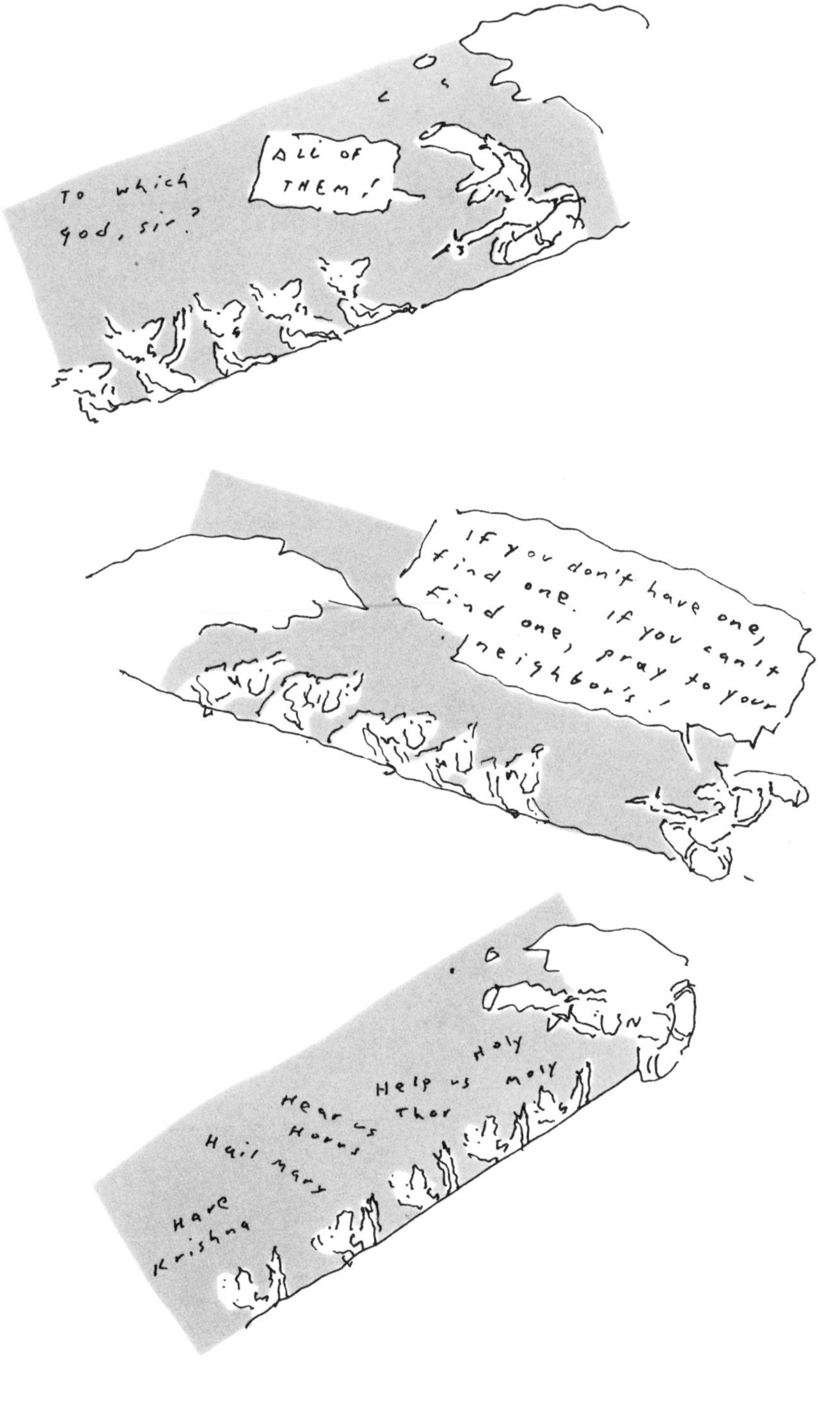
To which god, sir?
ALL OF THEM!
If you don't have one, find one. If you can't find one, pray to your neighbor's!
Holy Moly
Help us Thor
Hear us Horus
Hail Mary
Hare Krishna

it doesn't seem to be working!
It's that foreign wench!
THROW HER OVERBOARD !!
A first class passenger?!?
STOP!

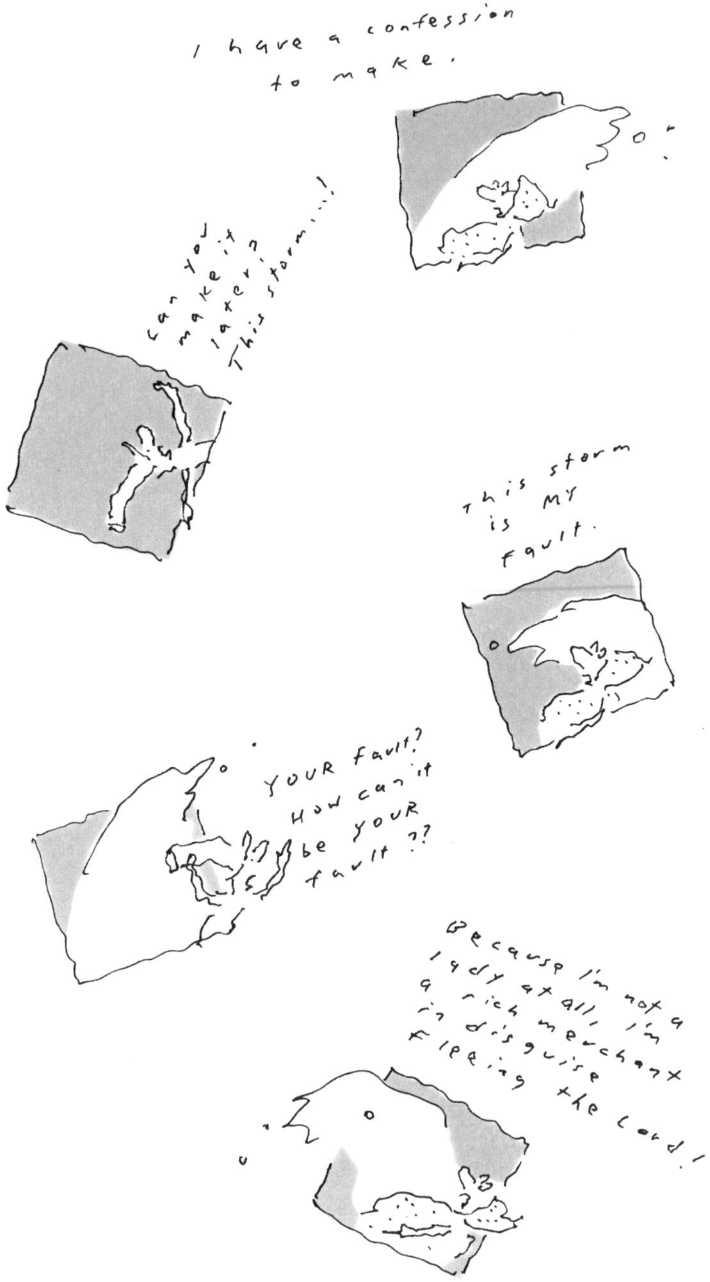
I have a confession to make.
Can you make it in This storm...!
This storm is MY fault.
YOUR fault? How can it be YOUR fault??
Because I'm not a lady at all! I'm a rich merchant in disguise fleeing the Lord!

THROW HER OVERBOARD!

There's no need to throw me overboard...

...I'll go myself.

Now which way is the sea?

Could you sign this waiver of liabilitti please?

OOPS.

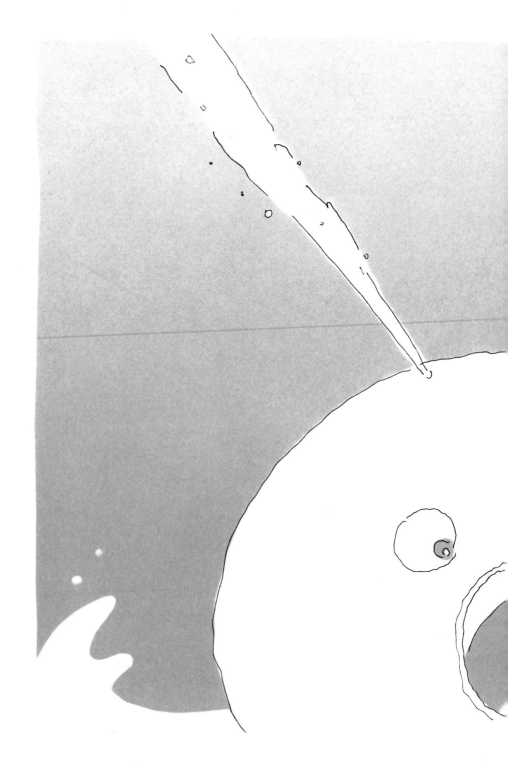

PART

THREE

It's dark in here.

smelly, too.

Oh, Lord, I know I have
disobeyed you.

I know I have
disguised myself
and tried to flee
your all-seeing gaze.
But listen...
just let me
out of here
and I'll do
Anything you want.
I promise,

Anything!

JONAH
SON OF AMITAI

IT IS I
THE LORD
YOUR GOD

GOD OF
THY FATHER
AND THY
FATHER'S
FARTHEST
FATHER

I HAVE COME
TO REMIND
THEE
GO TO
THE PEOPLE
OF NINEVEH
THAT
GREAT
CITY

AND CRY AGAINST IT FOR ITS WICKEDNESS.

ENJOY!

I should have taken the land route.
Brought my own food.
Meat... Lamb...
A Crown Roast
with stuffing.
Veggies
Beets
Acorn Squash with Honey
Brandied figs à la mode

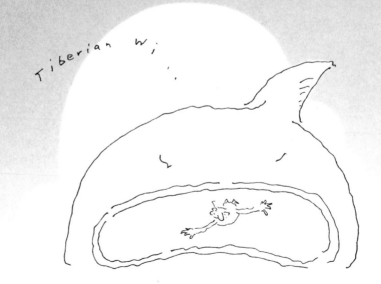

Tiberian W.

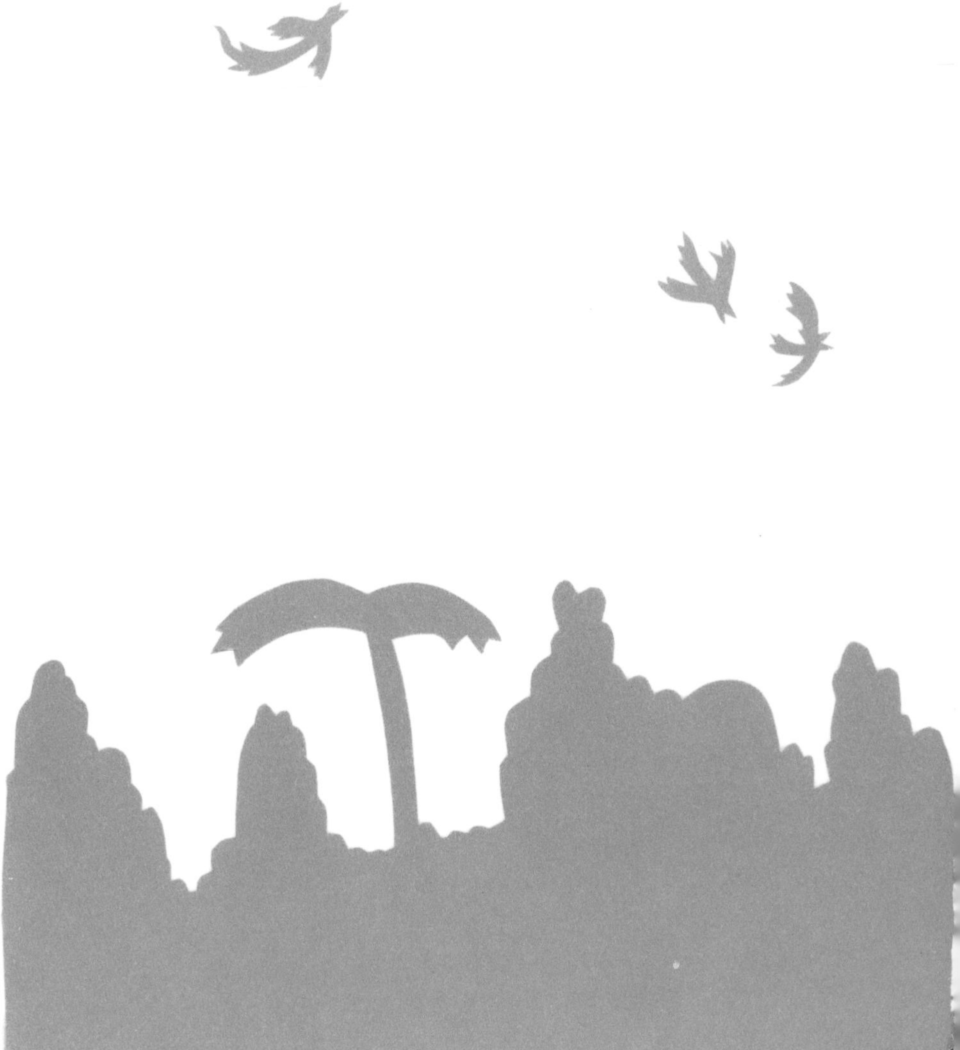

HALT!

no vagrants allowed in Nineveh!

I'm not a vagrant, officer, I'm a rich merchant from Nabatea en route to Tarshish but before I could reach my destination a hurricane struck and a whale swallowed me.
A storyteller, eh? pass.

But if I catch you begging, it's your HAND!

Terrible
place.

—worse
than home!

CLEAR THE WAY!
CLEAR THE WAY!
What is it?
THE IMPERIAL GUARD!
NO, IT MUST BE...

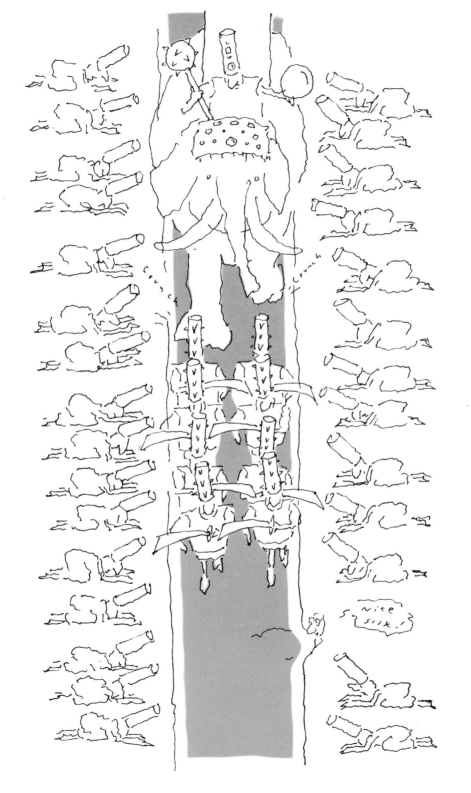

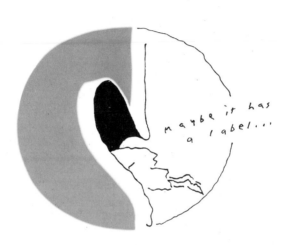

maybe it has
a label...

it's dark
in here.

JONAH!

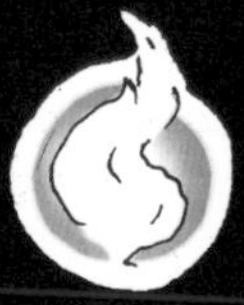

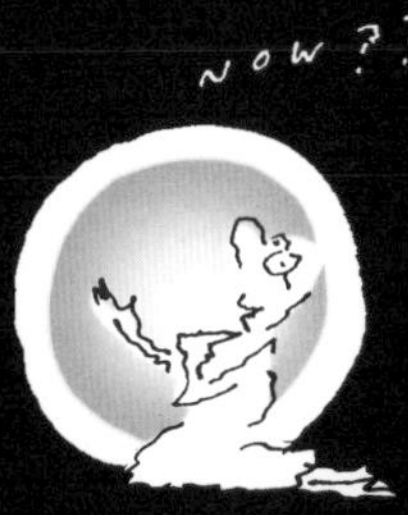
NOW??

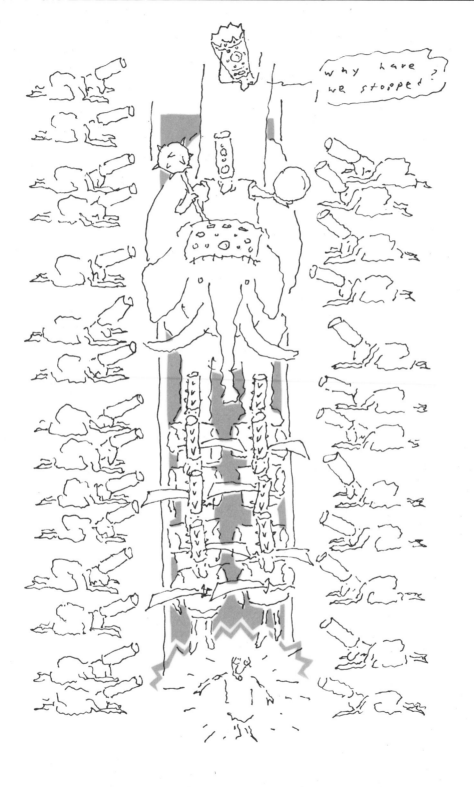

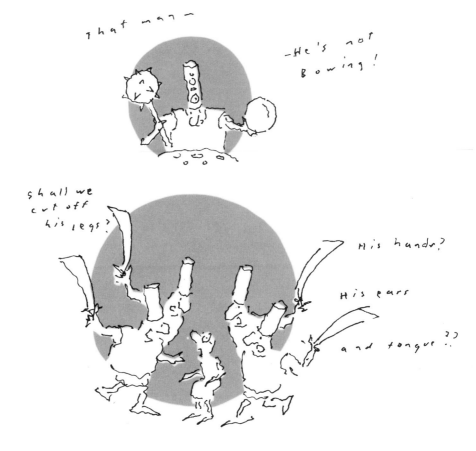

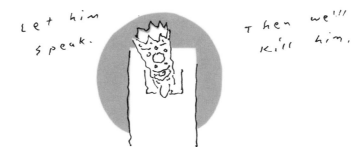

i'm a wealthy merchant from Nabutea en route to Tarshish but before i could reach my destination a terrible Hurricane struck and a Huge whale swallowed me and cast me on this shore.
Excellent. A storyteller. continue.
SOAP

I was sent by the Lord to cry out against the Wickedness of Nineveh!
SOAP

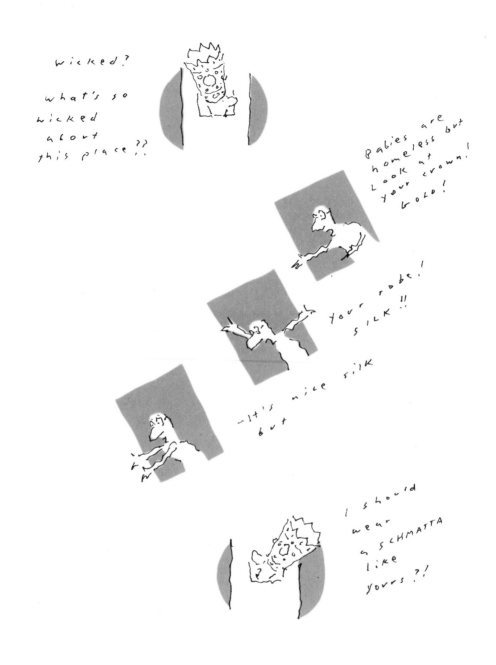

now, that wasn't
so difficult.

not a
bad king.

my foot!

Have to be back soon,
ship that order...

back....??

my
Back!

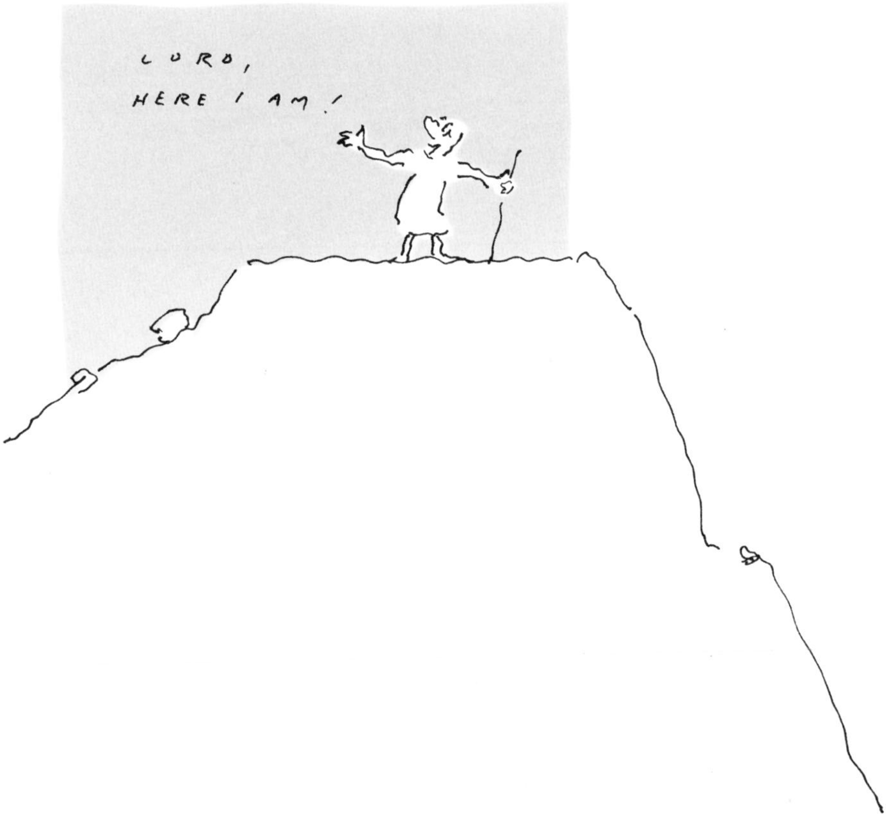
LORD,
HERE I AM!

THOU HAST

SPOKEN TO

NINEVEH.

JONAH!

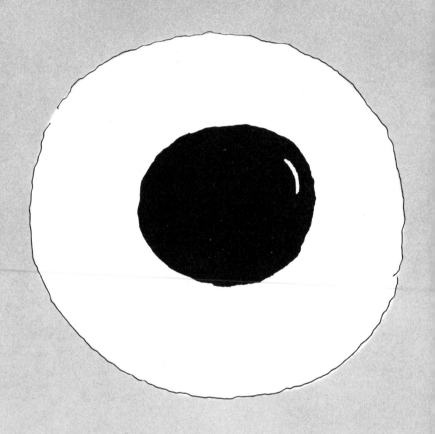

UTTERLY,

A BANDONED.

JONAH, THY
FAITHFUL SERVANT
HAS ACCOMPLISHED
THY MISSION.

Time to
bring me
back?

Lord ??

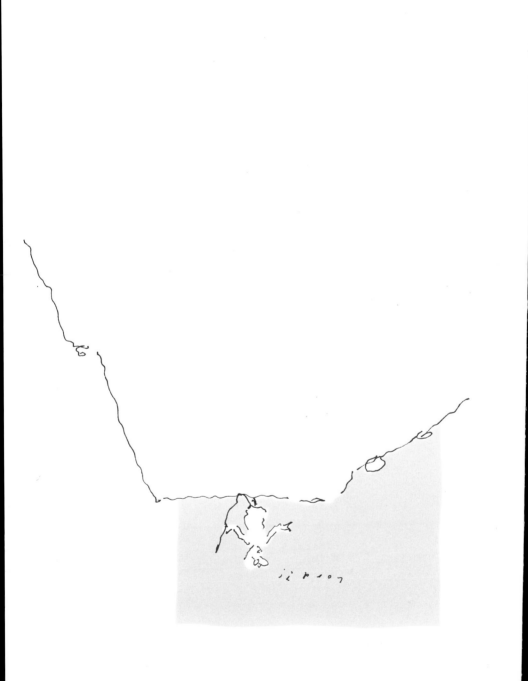

BUT THY WORDS
HAVE BEEN OF
FAINT TONGUE.

NOW

THE LORD

SHALL ACT.

BEHOLD

As

NOAH BEFORE

THEE,

WITNESS

THE LORD'S

WRATH.

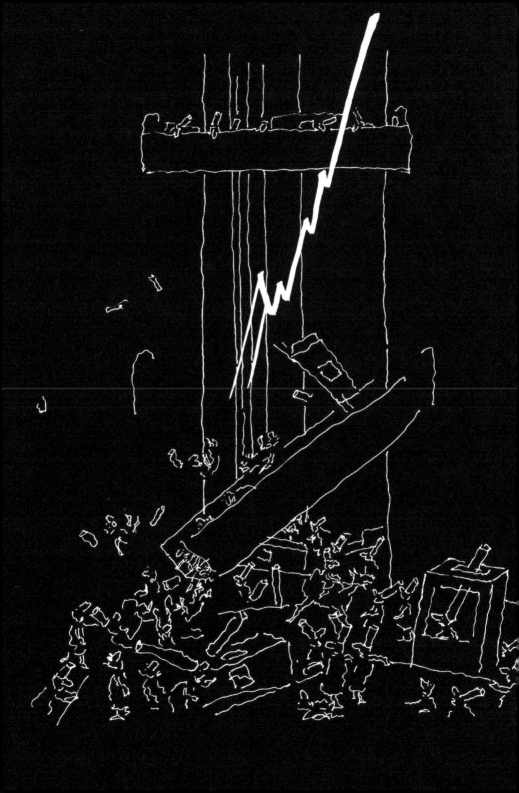

HIS
TWIN-TIPPED
LIGHTNING
BOLT

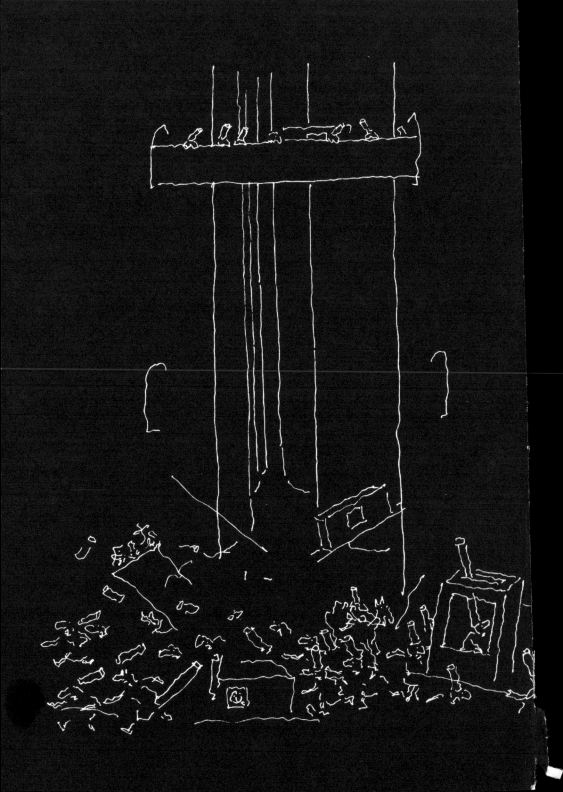

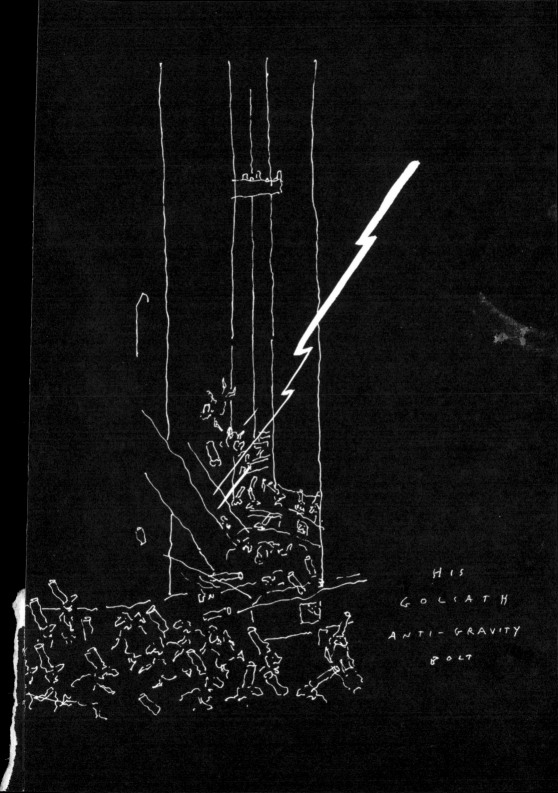

HIS
GOLIATH
ANTI-GRAVITY
BOLT

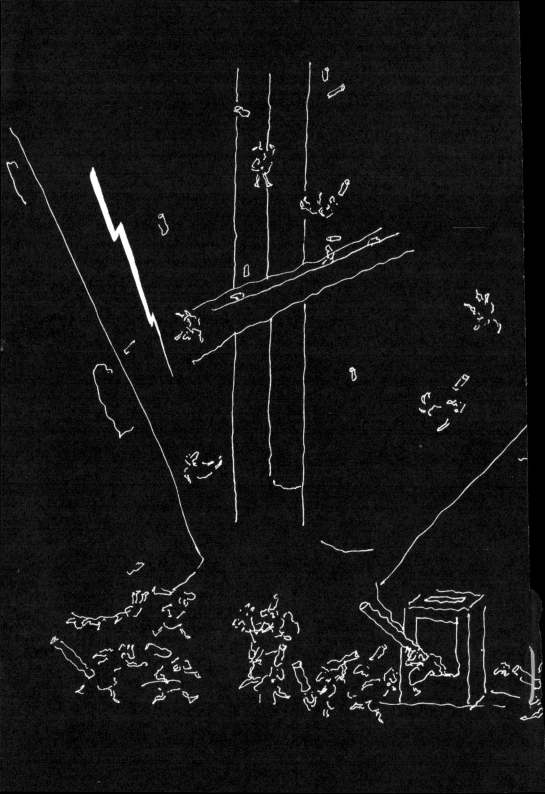

HIS
TOWER-OF-
BABEL-
BUSTERS

HIS
SMART-
SOLOMON

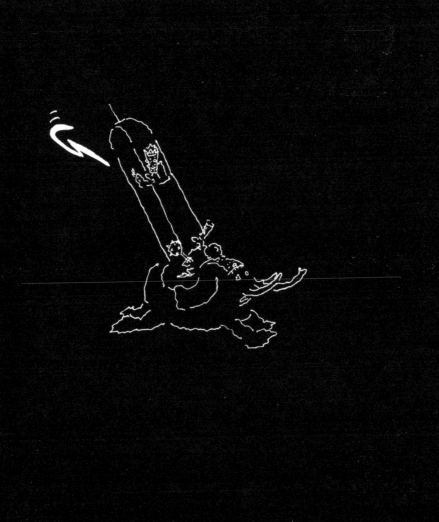

AND

FINALLY...

you haven't
touched your
soup.

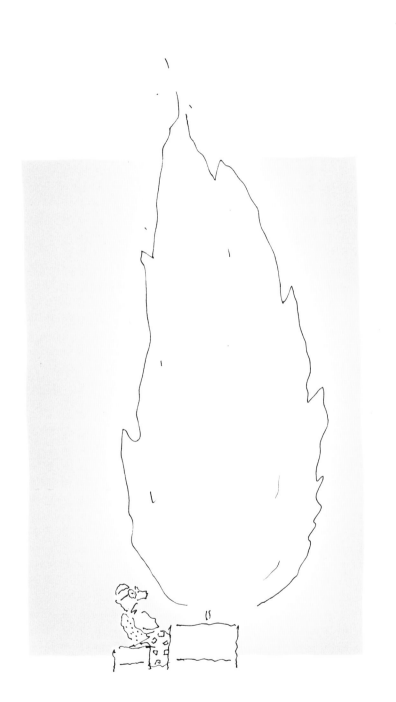